Top Notes

Nick Enright's

A Man With Five Children

Study notes for Standard English:
Module C 2015–2020 HSC

Bruce Pattinson

—— A ——
FIVE SENSES
PUBLICATION

Five Senses Education Pty Ltd
2/195 Prospect Highway
Seven Hills 2147
New South Wales
Australia

Pattinson, Bruce,
Top Notes – A Man with Five Children
ISBN 978-1-74130-998-0

CONTENTS

INTRODUCTION TO THE TOP NOTES SERIES

Top Notes are designed with the high school student in mind. They are written in an easy to read manner yet discuss the important ideas and issues needed to successfully undertake English HSC examinations.

They are written by teachers who have years of experience. Each Top Notes contains many helpful tips for the course and examination. Top Notes focus specifically on the student's needs and they examine each text in the context of the module and elective to which it has been allocated.

Each text includes:

- Notes on the specific module
- Plot summary
- Character analysis
- Setting
- Thematic concerns
- Language studies
- Essay questions and a plan
- Other textual material
- Additional questions
- Useful quotes

I am sure you will find these Top Notes useful in your studies of English.

Bruce Pattinson
Series Editor

THE STANDARD COURSE

This is a brief analysis of the Standard course to ensure you are completely familiar with requirements for the examination. If in any doubt at all, check with your teacher or the Board of Studies website.

The Standard Course requires you to have studied:

- Four prescribed texts. This means four texts from the list given to your teacher by the Board of Studies.

- For each of the texts, one must come from each of the following four categories.

  - drama
  - poetry
  - prose fiction (novel usually)
  - nonfiction or media or film or multimedia texts. (Multimedia are CD ROMs, websites, etc.)

- A range of related texts of your own choosing. These are part of your Area of Study, Module A and Module C. Do not confuse these with the main set text you are studying. This is very important.

Paper One

Area of Study: Discovery

Paper Two

Module A	*Module B*	*Module C*
Experience through Language	**Close Study of Text**	**Texts and Society**
Electives	*Electives*	*Electives*
▪ Distinctive Voices OR ▪ Distinctively Visual	▪ Drama OR ▪ Prose Fiction OR ▪ Nonfiction, Film, Media, Multimedia OR ▪ Poetry	▪ Exploring Interactions OR ▪ Exploring Transitions

You must study the Area of Study and EACH of Modules A, B and C

There are options within EACH of these that your school will select.

TEXTS AND SOCIETY

ELECTIVE ONE: Exploring Interactions

The "Texts and Society" module, Module C, requires you to examine and analyse texts which arise from or represent a particular situation or context. The syllabus states that, "Modules...emphasise particular aspects of shaping meaning and representation, questions of textual integrity, and ways in which texts are valued."[1] Texts and Society is a module that asks students to:

- Explore and analyse texts in a specific situation.

- Examine the ways texts communicate information, ideas, bodies of knowledge, attitudes and belief systems in ways particular to specific areas of society.

HSC PRESCRIPTIONS 2015-20 P14

The first elective in Texts and Society is Exploring Interactions. Exploring Interactions is the particular focus when studying *A Man with Five Children* by Nick Enright. The Module's focus must be kept in mind as well as the elective.

The idea of interactions should be explored in and through the text. That is, with reference to content and techniques. It can be explored thematically and can also relate to the characters, their interactions and the dynamics of relationships.

---

1   http://www.boardofstudies.nsw.edu.au/syllabus_hsc/pdf_doc/english-prescriptions-2015-20.pdf

Interactions should also be explored through the textual form, in this case, Enright's choice of drama script. In this way, the Module's mention of "Text" assumes significance. This focus on textual form and techniques holds true for your approach to, not only your prescribed text, but also your related text choices. Ask how the poetic, filmic, narrative, dramatic or other specific techniques linked to the textual form of your related material, contribute to representing interactions within the given text.

The rubric for this elective prescribes that,

"students explore and analyse a variety of texts that portray the ways in which individuals live, interact and communicate in a range of social contexts. These contexts may include the home, cultural, friendship and sporting groups, the workplace and the digital world. Through exploring their prescribed text and texts of their own choosing, students consider how acts of communication can shape, challenge or transform attitudes and beliefs, identities and behaviours. In their responding and composing, students develop their understanding of how the social context of individuals' interactions can affect perceptions of ourselves and others, relationships and society." HTTP://WWW.BOARDOFSTUDIES. NSW.EDU.AU/SYLLABUS_HSC/PDF_DOC/ENGLISH-PRESCRIPTIONS-2015-20.PDF

After studying this text, you will have,

- Analysed a variety of texts
- Explored how these texts portray the ways individuals live, interact and communicate in a range of social contexts.
- Understood that contexts may be personal, social, historical and cultural. They can include home,

friendship and sporting groups, the workplace and the digital world.

- Considered how acts of communication can shape, challenge and transform attitudes, beliefs, identities and behaviours.
- Developed an understanding of how the social context of interactions can affect perceptions of ourselves and others, relationships and society.

This module requires you to find other texts. The exam question for this module will usually ask you to write an essay, which would involve forming an answer to a specific essay question, and using your interpretation of the text(s) to draw conclusions about the essay subject.

The exam question will focus on the ideas in the rubric. Always remember that the focus must be on Exploring Interactions, textual forms and features and links to society.

Regardless of the questions you receive in your exams and assessments, your marks will improve if you can:

- Analyse and interpret the text instead of retelling
- Discuss the intentions of the composer(s) and the various effects on the responder
- Identify techniques and integrate an analysis of the effect of techniques into your response
- Keep a focus on the Module, Elective and discuss the interactions in the textual material and links between text and related material.

DRAMATIC TECHNIQUES

With this text there is a particular focus on language and theatre because it is drama. It is drama, however, that is linked with film and documentary and so there is interaction at a genre level. A key documentary device is the issue of selectivity and bias and this is worth considering in the play. The notion of intersecting genres is worthy of consideration in terms of your elective topic, Exploring Interactions. The interactions may be structural as well as content based. You should, by now, be familiar with language and dramatic features. Language features are the techniques that are used to create meaning. Dramatic techniques can be broken down into key areas:

1. **Visual:** features are predominantly made up of *mise-en-scene* or everything that appears on the stage. This includes the costumes, properties (props), make-up, lighting and the setting.

2. **Verbal:** the literary qualities of the dialogue and the delivery of the dialogue. This will be developed further in the language section of this study guide.

3. **Action:** includes the gestures the actors make and the blocking. Blocking refers to where the characters are standing, where they move on stage and why.

4. **Aural:** this element refers to everything that the audience hears separate to the dialogue. Aural features include sound effects and music.

5. **Theatrical:** theatrical features refer to the structural aspects of the play that are specific to the dramatic form. For

example, Shakespearean plays often contain soliloquies, asides, and sometimes tableaux and the 'play within the play'. Other theatrical features to consider are the number of acts, scenes and whether there are scene changes, or if the action is continuous. For example, Shakespeare's tragedies usually have five acts.

Regarding Action or technique three, in particular, the blocking will change depending on the type of stage on which the actors are performing. Stage types include -

- The proscenium arch stage

- The arena stage

- The open stage

- The traverse stage

- The thrust stage (Think of the Globe Theatre)

When examining blocking, it is also necessary to consider **proxemics**. Proxemics are the spatial relationships between characters. If two characters have an intimate relationship, then they would be positioned close together. The proxemics would, conversely, be different if a character is attempting to establish their authority over another. Proxemics and blocking are subsequently necessary when considering who has the focus during the scene. Focus is based on where the audience is looking on the stage. In a filmic text, such relationships are established through use of camera angles. It is imagined that in discussing interactions, this may well be a relevant technique to consider.

When considering how the action takes place on stage, you should also use the correct **stage geography**. The positions on the stage are taken from the perspective of the performer standing on the stage facing the audience.

- **Stage left (p)** is the left side of the stage in relation to the performer. Conversely it is the right side of the stage from the audience's perspective.

- **Stage right (op)** is on the right side of the performer on the stage or the left side of the stage from the audience's perspective.

- **Upstage** is actually the back of the stage, moving away from the audience.

- **Downstage** is the front of the stage towards the audience in a traditional proscenium arch stage.

After the ideas, forms and language of the text have been considered, also consider how the elements of the text itself interact and affect the audience. The Board of Studies also asks that you consider the way in which *A Man with Five Children* shows a number of social contexts and the communication and interactions that occur. Furthermore, you should consider how *A Man with Five Children* was produced within its original context and how it was presented i.e. How the ideas were communicated to the audience. Although they can be fairly creative, it is essential that productions of the play do not alter the meaning of the play significantly.

GRAPHIC COURTESY OF WIKIPEDIA PICTURES COMMONS CONTENT

STUDYING A DRAMA TEXT

The medium of any text is very important. If a text is a drama this must not be forgotten. Plays are not read they are viewed. This means you should never refer to the "reader" but the "audience" as the respondent to the text.

The marker will want to know you are aware of the text as a play and that you have considered its effect in performance.

Remembering a drama text is a play also means when you are exploring how the composer represents his/her ideas you MUST discuss dramatic techniques. This applies to any response using a drama text, irrespective of the form of the response.

Dramatic techniques are all the devices the playwright uses to represent his or her ideas. They are the elements of a drama that are manipulated by playwrights and directors to make any drama effective on stage! You might also see them referred to as dramatic devices or theatrical techniques. Some of these have been raised in the previous section.

Every play uses dramatic techniques differently. Some playwrights are very specific about how they want their play performed on stage. Others, like Shakespeare, give virtually no directions. They might give detailed comments at the beginning of the play and/or during the script. These are usually in italics and are called stage directions. They are never spoken but provide a guide to the director and actors about how the play is to appear and sound when performed.

Some common dramatic techniques are shown on the diagram that follows.

DRAMATIC TECHNIQUES

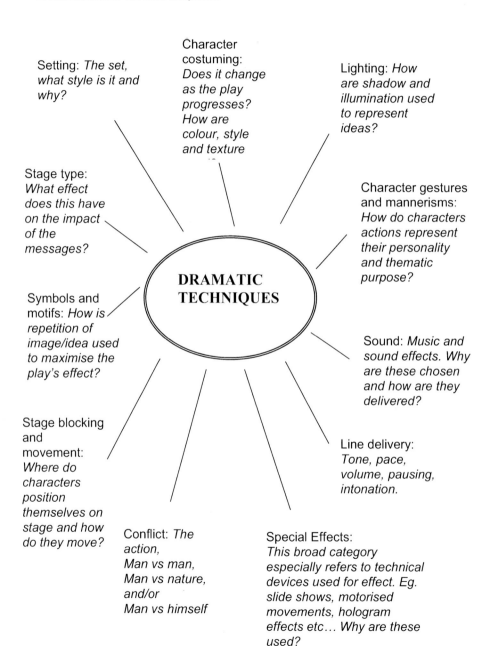

Setting: *The set, what style is it and why?*

Character costuming: *Does it change as the play progresses? How are colour, style and texture*

Lighting: *How are shadow and illumination used to represent ideas?*

Stage type: *What effect does this have on the impact of the messages?*

Character gestures and mannerisms: *How do characters actions represent their personality and thematic purpose?*

DRAMATIC TECHNIQUES

Symbols and motifs: *How is repetition of image/idea used to maximise the play's effect?*

Sound: *Music and sound effects. Why are these chosen and how are they delivered?*

Stage blocking and movement: *Where do characters position themselves on stage and how do they move?*

Line delivery: *Tone, pace, volume, pausing, intonation.*

Conflict: *The action, Man vs man, Man vs nature, and/or Man vs himself*

Special Effects: *This broad category especially refers to technical devices used for effect. Eg. slide shows, motorised movements, hologram effects etc… Why are these used?*

THE PLAYWRIGHT

Nick Enright: An Actor's Playwright by Pender and Lever (Eds) states,

> *'In A Man with Five Children, one of Enright's last plays, he explored his ideas about family and fate' (p22)*

This is relevant as Enright's play can be seen as an exploration of interactions and we can easily transpose this into our studies without forcing examples or content. Enright was a very important figure in Australian theatre, film and literature prior to his premature death. He left behind a large body of high quality work which was generally well received and critically respected.

Enright was born in 1950 and died in 2003 so his life and works are compressed into 53 years. Despite dying in his early fifties, as did the bard, Shakespeare, he achieved much. Enright achieved so much in fact, he was awarded an Order of Australia Medal posthumously for 'service to the performing arts, particularly as a playwright, teacher, actor, director, and as a mentor of emerging talent'.

There is a substantial amount of biographical material on Enright and if you need additional background and context for the author you can access the following sources which were accurate at the time of publication.

HTTP://WWW.LIVEPERFORMANCE.COM.AU/HALLOFFAME/NICKENRIGHT1.HTML

HTTP://WWW.IMDB.COM/NAME/NM0258012/BIO

HTTP://EN.WIKIPEDIA.ORG/WIKI/NICK_ENRIGHT

HTTP://WWW.AUSTLIT.EDU.AU/AUSTLIT/PAGE/A20517

It is also recommended that you read *The Man Behind the Camera* introductory notes and the Playwright's Note at the beginning of the Currency Press (2003) edition of the play which are helpful in placing the writing in context. While biographical detail is important, relevant and interesting, remember that it is the text itself on which you must focus.

PUTTING THE PLAY IN CONTEXT

7 Up and Reality Television

The series that was a catalyst for the development and production of the play you are studying was a series entitled *7 Up*. *7 Up* is usually associated with Michael Apted although he wasn't the first director. Paul Almond was the first director. The series is a longitudinal documentary study of a group of children and the series is now into the *56 Up* stage with a documentary film every seven years. You will find further explanation of the series and the origin of the idea for the play in the introductory notes.

The original series was designed to target a large cross section of English social strata with all economic classes involved. The series was underlined by the theory that future status and wealth was already predetermined by childhood status. Without going into the details, this theory played out in some ways. If you are interested, the series is readily available on the internet. What is more important to a study of this elective are the relationships these characters form. Some are still friends while others have now refused to participate. This is mirrored in the play. Also some of the criticisms of Gerry in the play are applicable to Apted in real life.

The Up series has been criticised by both ethnographers and the subjects themselves for its editing style. Mitchell Duneier has pointed out that Apted has the ability to assert causal relationships between a character's past and present that might not actually exist. Apted has acknowledged this fact, pointing out that in 21 Up he believed Tony would soon be in prison so he filmed him around dangerous areas for use in later films.

HTTP://FN.M.WIKIPEDIA.ORG/WIKI/UP_SERIES

This is reminiscent of Gerry's manipulative editing which is commented on by Enright through the text. The play also alludes to the origin of the series with the core idea being based on the Jesuit motto 'Give me a child until he is seven and I will give you the man.'

The question of why this social experiment was conducted is explored in the interactions between characters. The series also changed its tone from a political objective to a more personal analysis of the participants as time progressed. This is Gerry's progression as well and it changes much of the tone of the documentary.

For more information on the series use these sites:

HTTP://WWW.TELEGRAPH.CO.UK/CULTURE/CULTUREPICTUREGALLERIES/9259901/FROM-SEVEN-TO-56-UP-THE-STORY-SO-FAR.HTML

HTTP://WWW.NPR.ORG/2013/07/26/205760044/MICHAEL-APTED-AGING-WITH-THE-7-UP-CREW

HTTP://WWW.NEWYORKER.COM/CULTURE/CULTURE-DESK/WHAT-56-UP-REVEALS

These give the best insights that will assist you to understand the concept of the play and the nature of the interactions you are being asked to explore. These will also highlight that few interactions occur outside some social influence as well as the impositions provided by the media. This is emphasised in the criticisms of reality television, which the series is a part of, and these criticisms are transposed into the play,

'The authenticity of reality television is often called into question by its detractors. The genre's title of "reality" is often criticised as being inaccurate because of claims that the genre frequently includes elements such as premeditated scripting, acting, urgings from behind-the-scenes crew to create specified situations of adversity and drama and misleading editing.'

While the idea for the play is contained within this longitudinal study, the characters in the play are fictitious and the play is based in Australia rather than the UK.

PLOT OUTLINE

We begin to discover each of the children as individuals

The children meet at the zoo

Gerry becomes involved when he should be objective

Gerry sees much promise in Jessie

Cameron comes to be great at Aussie Rules

Susannah is academically successful and sleeps with Gerry

Zoe becomes typecast as 'dumb' by the filming and editing

Roger is typecast as a rich spoilt kid, especially at his 21st

Jessie and Theo have a slowly developing relationship

Zoe has a child with a singer and Doug takes on the responsibility of the family

Cameron marries Annie, has kids and success but loses it in the accident

Susannah comes back from overseas pregnant and has a daughter

Roger goes away to find himself and is murdered by terrorists

Zoe becomes confident

Jessie, the crusader for causes, has a miscarriage, then gets cancer and dies while being filmed

The children go off to celebrate Jessie's life without Gerry

We end with Gerry in the camera frame admitting he lived through the children

PLOT SUMMARY

Act One
Scene One

Gerry (Gerald Hilferty) begins on a bare stage where he is explaining what he wants. His idea is to take one day out of the lives of five children, and he promises the parents they will have a record of their child's life. Roger Chan, the first of the children, comes to Gerry and asks him why he is doing this but before he can answer we meet the other children; Jessie, Cam (Cameron), Susannah and Zoe. We learn from the scene, as they move off, some of the qualities and background of each child. Cam swears and is racist, Roger is intelligent and privileged, Susannah is proper and formal while Jessie is of Aboriginal descent. Gerry tries to keep the peace as they interact for the first time. One important stage prop to note is Gerry's ubiquitous camera which becomes more and more important as the play progresses.

The children are seven years old when the film begins. They talk to the camera where we see, through visual and auditory cues, their socio-economic differences, educational levels and ambitions for the future. Susannah sings a French song which means roughly translated,

> In the moonlight, my friend Pierrot,
> Lend me your pen to write a word,
> My candle is dead; I no longer have fire,
> Open your door, for the love of God to me.

Scene Two

It is now 1975 and we are at a children's home. Cam is going to live with his aunt and uncle as his mother has died but he wants to live with Gerry. We can see Cam's attachment to Gerry and Gerry promises to take him to the football. The scene ends with a hug.

Scene Three

It is 1977 and Roger is on the floor playing with a Star Wars figurine of Obi Wan Kenobe and playing out a *Star Wars: A New Hope* scene.

Scene Four

Zoe and Jessie are thirteen (1978) and talk about their limited sexual experiences when they share a filmed kiss. Jessie warns Gerry that one day someone will sneak up on him.

Scene Five

It is still 1978 and Susannah is highlighting her intelligence by displaying and explaining a dissected frog. She mentions poetry and asks the frog, 'How do you think it felt?'

Scene Six

Jessie is fourteen now and she begins to read a message about weapons to make a point but Gerry says it's boring and prompts her to talk about something with passion or about her experience as 'Young black Australia'. She is enthused by Gerry who convinces her she is a leader and she makes a speech off camera at the end of the scene.

Scenes Seven and Eight

The split scene (1979) occurs as Zoe and Susannah are in separate places when they hear Gerry's speech about Jessie's speech in the Domain. Zoe is now very different from Susannah who is successful academically. Zoe sees herself as 'ordinary' and Susannah admits to writing poetry. The scene ends with the ominous foreshadowing of Gerry saying, 'You can stop anytime'.

Scene Nine

The 1980 edition credit roll and all the kids dialogue is [on screen]. Cam is all about football and thinks he 'must be missing something'. He lives with his auntie and uncle who don't like him and he doesn't like them. Susannah is focussed on academia and literature, Zoe is uncertain about her life while Roger, the one born on Australia Day, wants much materially from life. Jessie says at the end, after the replay of her kiss with Zoe says 'I want time to be all the things that I can be. None of us want that time taken from us. We want our chance at life.'

Scene Ten

Here the five review the show from the previous scene and Jessie is aware enough to realise Gerry is manipulating what is seen. He says he will follow them until they are twenty-one but Jessie says this was an agreement he had with their parents, not them. Cam and Roger argue and Cam resorts to violence and racist comments. Despite this Susannah thinks they are a family and Jessie thinks they should have some rules to which Gerry agrees. He gets Zoe to bring Cam back and Gerry then tells Roger how hard Cam's life is though he is excelling at Aussie Rules, a game

Roger doesn't understand. The conclusion to the scene has Cam and Roger explaining how and what they are and Roger says Gerry was supposed to take him to the football too.

Scene Eleven

It is 1981 and Cam is coming out of a police station after having stolen a car. He wants now to live with Gerry and he agrees if Cam stops the drugs, gets a job and begins training again. Cam agrees to let him shoot him coming out of the 'cop shop' in return.

Scene Twelve

Roger (17) is alone on screen in 1982 and says his father's expectations of him have fallen but he likes the idea of being a student despite not knowing what to study.

Scene Thirteen

Zoe is also seventeen in 1982 and Gerry finds her working in a supermarket after having left school. She has moved in with a band and she likes the changes in her life. Gerry thinks she should be in school and he doesn't want her to waste her life. Despite this she doesn't want to leave the project and she finishes on screen describing her life as having just kicked in 'big time'.

Scene Fourteen

We are in the backyard of Susannah's house in December of 1983. Gerry has arrived after having returned from Borneo to give her a present for her success in the final exams. She now plans to be a doctor. She is more confident in herself and allows Gerry to shoot her reading poetry but his battery gives out before she is finished.

Scene Fifteen

It is 1984 and at Zoe's house she and Jessie are looking at Gerry's photos of Borneo. Jessie is enthused but not Zoe who doesn't want to go to Borneo to save the world and have Gerry film it. In this scene we meet Doug who becomes important as the plot progresses. They again come back to the 'kiss' from years before and even Doug knows about it.

Scene Sixteen

Cam is playing footy in the winter of 1984 and Gerry is in the crowd with Cam's girlfriend, Annie. Roger arrives and thinks Annie is with Gerry. Gerry films Roger with Annie but Roger isn't there to be filmed. The scene ends with Cam in triumph on the field.

Scene Seventeen

We are now in December of 1985 and Gerry is with Susannah in her flat. Susannah has done brilliantly again and yet she wants to talk about the time she read her poetry. She admits that she loved Gerry at eighteen but is over it now which is why she now can ask him to 'fuck' her. She hasn't even had a boyfriend and yet she grabs him and says it'll be a secret. He succumbs to her desire and the scene concludes with a kiss.

Scene Eighteen

Zoe has a baby and she is now twenty. It is 1985 and she is telling the camera how happy she is being married to Doug. Doug is also happy even though he has dropped out of law to look after Zoe and Sky.

Scene Nineteen

Still in 1985 we are outside a restaurant where Cam is calling Annie out to propose to her. He tells her he has been selected by Essendon and will be moving to Melbourne. He asks her to go with him and he proposes. She has conditions but accepts as Gerry films, even though she has told him to 'piss off'.

Scene Twenty

Jessie is now telling the camera about herself at the end of 1985. She says she is in lots of relationships but her activism is more important. She is 'Just Jessie' and likes her life. She asks Gerry 'Do you like your life?' But he edits this out.

Scene Twenty-one

It is Australia Day 1986 and we begin with Theo and Jessie talking and we know Theo is interested in Jessie but is put off by her imposing reputation and public persona. She says she doesn't want a boyfriend but will take a free meal off him. Before he can get her home Gerry arrives to take her to Roger's 21st birthday party at the Regent.

Scene Twenty-two

The whole five original children plus Doug, Annie and Gerry are together at Zoe's house on Australia Day 1987 watching the latest and supposedly last, instalment of the series. Roger is on screen talking about his life, the fourteen years of filming and Gerry's involvement. Roger is then given the sports area he has always wanted. Susannah says she thinks it is odd to leave the series at this point when they all have so much ahead of them. The telecast ends with Jessie saying 'We just want our chance at life.'

They toast something new and Gerry then goes into a long speech about how it is not the time to stop but there is more to show about their life journey. He says another decade would be good and leaves the room to let them decide. Roger is against the idea but the others think it might be fun and convince him to participate. Susannah thinks she will be a 'shadow' if she doesn't and concludes the scene 'There we are. Five blind mice. See how they run.'

Scene Twenty-three

Gerry is at Cam's post award footy party. He assists him to cheat on a pregnant Annie with a blonde who he met at the awards. Cam tells Gerry that he always gets him the 'good stuff' on film.

Scene Twenty-four

Roger is now twenty-three and it is 1988. He is still uncertain about what he is to be and it seems he just wants to escape from what he is and his background. He comes across as insecure despite his privileged upbringing.

Scene Twenty-five

It is 26th January 1988 and we are at Jessie's house as she and Theo are preparing for a march. Theo does not want to be in Gerry's film and he says Gerry should concentrate in the Koori aspects of the day. He also informs Gerry that he and Jessie are not a couple and she has no room for him in her life as he came too late into it.

Scene Twenty-six

Zoe is speaking in 1989 and she states that she has continued with the show because of her daughter. She wants to show her that her mum is going somewhere and she doesn't remember the girl who said she wasn't going anywhere.

Scene Twenty-seven

It is 1989 and Gerry and Roger are jogging along a beach on the coast of New South Wales. Roger is happy to be at the beach and out of the city. He says the world is Gerry's natural environment whereas he doesn't fit in anywhere. He has broken with his father and lost nearly half a million dollars. He is snorting cocaine and needs a break. Roger wants to stay with Gerry but Gerry hesitates to let him and they hash over the past. Roger thinks Gerry has set him up, especially by showing the Maserati on his twenty-first birthday. Roger guesses he 'fucked' Susannah and how Roger has his own role. Gerry promises to help Roger if he can go and 'test himself'. Gerry promises to come when Roger sends him a sign, albeit with the camera.

Scene Twenty-eight

It is now 1989 and Gerry is filming Susannah in her graduation gown. Susannah has changed her mind and she is going to follow paediatrics rather than psychiatry. She sings 'My candle is dead, I no longer fire' and makes Gerry put the camera away. She wonders what happened to 'them' and why he left her when she genuinely loved him. She says her once a year effort for him is a valentine, a 'once a year love letter on screen.' The playwright suggests an image of Jessie on the stage screen here.

Scene Twenty-nine

We are in 1990 at Jessie's house. Gerry says the street had become 'gentrified' and that he has just dropped in to see her, not to film. He says how hard it is for him to see her now after all those years, because of how much she has changed. It is her story that kept growing. He admits that he loves her and probably always has. He tells her he will even give up the project for her but she reveals that she is having a baby with Theo. They were mates but they moved on and then Theo enters. He is excited about the baby and says not even Gerry could have made him cool at fourteen like he did Jessie. He goes out and Jessie kisses Gerry asking if he would have really given up the project. Zoe enters and is excited and then Doug says Jessie is 'glowing' and notices Gerry has no camera. At this point Gerry leaves saying he has to be somewhere else. Jessie goes to follow but 'changes her mind.' The Act ends with images of the five children coming to rest on Jessie.

End of Act One

Questions for Act One

- Gerry opens the play by talking to the audience as they are the parents. What effect on the audience might this have in a theatre?

- Analyse what we learn about each of the five children in the longish opening scene. Why is this scene longer? Think about orientating the audience in your response.

- Describe your impression of each of the children up to Scene Six 1979.

- Discuss how you see Gerry at the early stages of the play. What are his motivations? Do you feel he is manipulative of the children or genuinely interested?

- At this early stage of the play how do we know Gerry is most attracted to Jessie?

- How significant is the kiss between Jessie and Zoe?

- Read Scene Eleven again. What is the dynamic between Cam and Gerry?

- In Scene Thirteen what element of society does Zoe represent? How do perceive Gerry's response to her decisions?

- Susannah is the most successful academically of the children. How is this shown in the play? Why does Enright make much of her interest in poetry? How do you see the scene where she and Gerry have sex? Is he taking advantage of her neediness or is there more to the relationship?

- Discuss the relationship between Zoe and Doug throughout the first Act.

- Chart how Cam's life changes throughout Act One.

- Why doesn't Gerry allow Roger to stay with him at the beach when he is obviously needy? Does this change your opinion of Gerry? As part of your response discuss your thoughts on why Roger is so needy and ineffective in life despite all the benefits he grew up with.

- Why does Gerry leave after his admission of love for Jessie at the end of the Act? Does this change our opinion of Gerry? Do you think he really would have stopped the series?

- Predict what might happen in the next Act based on your initial reading of Act One.

Act Two
Scene Thirty

Roger walks in Gerry's dream. Roger is calling for Gerry but he doesn't reveal where he is.

Scene Thirty-one

It is 1991 and we are outside a nightclub in Melbourne. Cam is chasing Zoe and wanting to have sex with her but Gerry intervenes and Zoe tells him she is in Melbourne for a funeral. Her old boyfriend, Alex, has died of AIDS. She also reveals Jessie lost her baby. She tells Gerry to get Cam home before he does 'real damage' and Cam insists he drive Gerry home so he can explain what Zoe meant.

Scene Thirty-two

The next night at Zoe and Doug's house they are discussing how Alex was the real father of Sky. Zoe wants to tell her and Doug says he has given up a lot to be her father. The dialogue is interrupted by a television news report of a car crash. Cam is in a critical condition and it says Gerry was also injured in the accident. We see Cam on screen over time talking about footy and the scene concludes with Zoe saying 'No more death. Please.'

Scene Thirty-three

Gerry and Susannah talk in 1993 and Gerry is walking with the aid of a stick. They talk of Cam and Annie and how they will cope. They also speak of Roger but little has been heard of him since Gerry told him to go and find himself. Susannah fills in the gaps since she last saw Gerry and then admits she is pregnant and wants Gerry to film.

Scene Thirty-four

Gerry works alone editing Susannah's speech about her life and pregnancy but edits the last section where she asks him if he is enjoying his life.

Scene Thirty-five

It is 1993 and we are in the backyard of Cam and Annie's house in Sydney. Life has changed for them both and Cam is in a wheelchair. Annie and Gerry are close and she asks him to take the kids out for activities. She assures Gerry that the family will be 'okay'.

Scene Thirty-six

1993 – Jessie and Theo are on screen but Jessie speaks. She says she is putting her energy into causes not kids as she can't have her own.

1994 – Gerry has Doug and Zoe on camera and we can now see a shifting dynamic as Doug has lost his job and can't go back and do law as they don't have the money. Zoe is looking for work so he can.

Scene Thirty-seven

We are at Susannah's house in 1994 and Zoe is going to care for Susannah's daughter, Gabrielle, as a job so Doug can go back to school. Gerry has worked out that Doug is not the father of Sky and wants the full story but Zoe is very reluctant and worried about the effect on Sky as she doesn't know. She says Gerry is the only one who wants to know the full story.

Scene Thirty-eight

Roger again enters Gerry's dream. He calls for Gerry without his camera and Gerry replies, 'I wouldn't be me without a camera.'

Scene Thirty-nine

We are at Gerry's house in 1995 and Roger is sitting beside him 'echoing' the newsreader who tells of how Roger and four compatriots were captured by rebels outside the Buddhist temple where they were living. They are hostages and will be released only if rebel leaders are released.

Scene Forty

It is now 1995 and Jessie and Theo are arguing at their house. He says she is a 'cause junkie' and she says it is about her people. He tells her she is really Gerry's 'girlfriend' and that she won't come back to him, there will always be another cause. Gerry arrives and tells of the rebels and how they executed each of the prisoners. Gerry was there but they haven't found Roger yet. Theo bitterly asks him if he filmed it and then leaves. Jessie then tells him she is going off the grid and won't be available for a year. Roger calls out to Gerry that Gerry didn't find him and the scene ends with Susannah singing her song again.

Scene Forty-one

Cam is talking to Gerry about how bright he, Cam, was as a child, just like his son. Annie comes in and says the kids have had a great day with Gerry. Gerry tells them Roger has not been found yet. He also has an offer for them to do a story for a women's magazine that will make them thirty five thousand. Annie says if she gets Cam to agree, they'll do it. Annie then says she and Gerry will go sky-diving for her thirtieth birthday as a thank you to Gerry.

Scene Forty-two

Zoe is thirty and the year is 1996. She is outside a nightclub telling her story on screen. She tells how she is getting on with her education and tonight she just wants to party.

Scene Forty-three

It is 1996 at Susannah's house and she and Zoe are arguing about the development of Susannah's child and Gerry is there as support. Susannah fires Zoe and contends she is having an affair with Gerry. He is offended that Susannah suggests he is after their children. Susannah goes off into a tangent of abuse that has some truths and Gerry is reasoned when he says she knows something is wrong with Gabrielle. Susannah says she never wants to hear from him again.

Scene Forty-four

The scene is set in a suburban ballet school where Doug and Gerry watch Sky dance. Doug says that she now knows she has had two fathers and is good with it. Zoe comes in and Doug is annoyed she has given permission for Gerry to film their daughter. He warns Gerry not to talk to her and says he doesn't want his life broadcast. He tells Gerry at the end they will only have family snaps from now on as the family is his work.

Scene Forty-five

Jessie is in Weipa at thirty-two years of age (1998) and has stayed there despite her protestations to Theo. He has visited but returned to the city. She has gone back but returned to Weipa. She states that she will go back 'soon'.

Scene Forty-six

Roger again walks into Gerry's dream and Gerry questions why. Roger says Gerry will work it . He will work out how to finish the film despite everyone not wanting to be filmed anymore and that's when he will work out why he enters Roger's dreams.

Scene Forty-seven

Gerry is drinking with Annie in the backyard in 1998. He is talking to her about how he can engineer the five to complete the film but she wants to talk about the affair they are having. She says it has to stop and then Cam, who has been watching them, says he knows. They argue and Cam finally admits Gerry was shooting in the car the night they crashed. Annie is shocked and asks Gerry if it was his fault. Cam concludes by telling how he made a deal with the devil and that devil was Gerry and he is still paying for it.

Scene Forty-eight

We are in Jessie and Theo's backyard on the 26 January 2000. Roger is sitting in the yard and Jessie can sense him. Doug arrives with Zoe, then Susannah, followed by Cam and Annie. They discuss Roger and then Gerry arrives. He asks permission to film and they all shrug or shake their heads. They agree today is the end and that most won't talk. Jessie is going to undergo chemotherapy and she is happy to have Gerry follow her. Her aim is to be there for her birthday in December. This longish scene ends with a reprise of her comment, 'I want time to be all the things I can be. None of us want that time taken from us. We want our chance at life.'

Scene Forty-nine

It is only a week later and we are in open space near water. The five are there including Roger. Theo sees Gerry coming with his camera and tells him to stop shooting. Theo also wants him to destroy the footage he shot at the hospital but Gerry refuses so he remains behind with Roger. Roger tells him to finish it but Gerry doesn't know how so he takes the camera and begins to film Gerry. He begins again and he begins to ask again to be part of their lives but now finishes with the idea that 'I'd like them to live for me.' The five children end the play why asking 'But why?'

THE END

Questions for Act Two

- What was the most important event in this Act for you? Explain your response fully.

- Why does Roger seem to haunt Gerry throughout the Act?

- Discuss how Zoe changes and develops over the course of the Act. How important an influence is Doug in her life?

- Do you think Gerry becomes too involved in the lives of the children? Discuss your response with detailed analysis of TWO of the characters in the text. You might wish to discuss one character such as Annie outside the five children.

- Analyse why Enright includes the scenes where Gerry cuts the footage.

- Do you think Theo is correct when he says that Gerry cast Jessie 'as a heroine' when she was fourteen?

- The children, as adults, can stop the filming and the series whenever they want. Why don't they? What do you think draws them always back into the series despite their own reservations and those of their partners?

- Is Jessie's cancer and death a surprise in the context of the play or has it been foreshadowed?

- Re-read the final dozen lines. Do you think the conclusion is suitable in the context of the play as a whole? Is it important Gerry goes back to when he was seven? Is it right to ask why?

- Which character was your favourite and why?

- Which character was your least favourite and why?

- Finally discuss your initial reaction on completing a reading of the play.

SETTING

The setting of the scenes is flexible in this play as it is set over an extended period of time. Before proceeding with this section, look back over the notes on staging in the earlier sections so that you have an idea of theatrical processes. Obviously, the play cannot have the 'normal' staging as the settings are widespread, such as a Melbourne nightclub to a suburban backyard, a headland and a beach. With constant changes it cannot be full stage changes. As Enright points out in his Note at the beginning, the 'technological demands' of the play are heavy and much is conveyed through this.

To give you an idea of the very minimalist settings of the play look at the graphics interspersed throughout the Currency edition of the Sydney Theatre Company production in 2002. The main idea we get of this production as far as setting goes is the large screen that dominates the background. Setting in this production is delineated by props such as the bed, the camera, a bench so it is very different from a conservative production with backgrounds painted and extensive set designs. Remember too, in some instances the actual place is not mentioned as it is irrelevant such as in scene three where 'Roger 12 plays with a figure of Obi Wan Kenobe'.

As the children become older, move out into the world and go their separate ways, the settings become relevant. They highlight specific events that illustrate personal traits of the character and are dramatic enough for Gerry to film such as Cam at the police station, the beach scene and the nightclub. Most of the scenes, however, because they are character based, have a vague setting such a as backyard or appear on screen.

Many of the scenes can be represented by a simple prop so the screen shots can be pre-prepared. I feel that this was Enright's intention because the concept of the play revolves around the camera and filming for presentation of character as seen, shot and importantly edited by Gerry. It is the exploration of the characters that is key. The setting only highlights what they are doing. An example of this is the backyard scenes that are so typical of Australia where events evolve that show both communication and miscommunication according to what individuals bring to the conversation. We are certainly never distracted by setting and it is the ubiquitous camera that dominates the stage. As Enright points out in his Notes, 'the film-maker is the subject.' We can see that it is his reaction to the children and eventually their children and partners that often shapes events.

My main focus here is to reinforce the idea that this is a play and when we explore interactions, the focus is on the characters on stage, not the setting which has a supporting role. When you write on this think about how the setting helps convey events and interactions rather than affecting characters deeply. As always, there is one exception which may be the scene where Jessie speaks from Weipa where her Indigenous connection to the land is relevant. You might also like to think about how you might portray the dream sequences where Roger seems to haunt Gerry. Setting forms a background for the focus on characters and their interactions.

QUESTIONS ON THE SETTING

- In your own words use ten lines to describe the theatre space where the play might take place. You can base your ideas on the graphics in the set text.

- What is so special about this play that the setting doesn't have to be defined to a place or time?

- What effect does setting have on the play in terms of being able to build and develop the interactions between characters?

- Describe what effect having a screen on stage has on the characters in the play. Think about how the characters are instructed to watch the screen during the play as their lives evolve.

- How does the setting help focus attention on the nature of Gerry's film-making?

CHARACTER ANALYSIS

Gerry

Gerry is the protagonist of the play and also the antagonist in many ways. Perhaps we can say that, as the central character who brings the others together, he is definitely pivotal in their lives. Gerry also controls the action of the play through the camera. We see his bias, not only in the manner of his interaction with the characters but the ways in which he affects their lives. In many ways, and we shall explore this idea further, Gerry lives his own life through his subjects in such a way that he is trapped in continuing, just as they are trapped in being filmed. Consider the choice of title in relation to the above point. Do you think the title supports the point?

Gerry opens the play with a lengthy appeal, beginning with the line 'I want your child' and this is echoed in the final scene when Roger forces Gerry to begin again with the line. So I think it is fair to say that Gerry begins his filming with good intentions and he makes this clear,

> 'Five people to speak for young Australia. I hope all five will want to come with me on the journey. (p1)

Gerry does take all of them on a journey but it is one which he influences, both directly and indirectly. He sleeps with Susannah, falls in love with Jessie, rescues Cam by letting him live with him and he sleeps with Annie, Cam's wife, rejects Roger and sends him away to find himself and portrays Zoe in a manner that pigeonholes her for a major portion of her life. Rather than an objective documentary, the journey becomes a subjective analysis of their lives, tinged with bias and shown clearly in the scenes where Gerry edits footage. He becomes preoccupied with the show and the children and, at times, adopts the role of a surrogate parent without the responsibility. When the initial decade is over he seeks more,

> *'I look around this group tonight and I'm thinking, who did I sell short? What did I miss? Where did I skimp?...We could show that every one of you is on the same journey, the one we're all on. But that will take time.' (p.33)*

Gerry is convincing and they agree, albeit reticently to continue for another ten years. They are his experiment in many ways yet the experimenter becomes part of the experiment. Gerry is the father figure to the group yet he has no substantive qualifications for this and hides behind the camera, using it as a prop. His obsession with filming breaks privacy, becomes intrusive and even leads to Cam's accident which leaves him in a wheelchair. He becomes overt in his desire to map each moment of their lives. He even films Jessie dying, and then refuses to edit it when Theo requests it. He is convinced they need to 'Wrap it up' but it is never ending. At the end he is left alone with Roger as the others move away. They leave him because of his refusal and then it turns full cycle as Roger begins to shoot Gerry as he admits,

> *'I'd like them to live for me.' (p.78)*

It can be said the play is all about Gerry, not about the children. The title echoes this through the syntax. It is not about "The Five Children and a Man" but rather, "A Man with Five Children". The foregrounding of "A Man", gives Gerry preeminence. He is omnipresent and he comes to live his life through them, especially Cam and Jessie. He breaks down the barrier that should exist and becomes part of their lives, at a cost. It is interesting though that the children still allow him to be around and film, despite their obvious displeasure at him. They certainly feel a strong connection to him despite being aware of what he is doing to them. Cam says it clearly in the words,

> *'I did a deal with the devil. And it's you. You're the devil. We did our deal and now I'm paying for it. And I'll keep paying, won't I? Won't I Gerry? Body and soul.' (p.72)*

As an audience we need to decide how we see Gerry as a character. He can be a master manipulator whose cinematic interventions change lives yet he can also be well meaning and vulnerable. He appears to live his life more and more through the five subjects yet as this occurs he changes their lives. Certainly Gerry is flawed and his connection with them finally breaks after Jessie's death. Is it the fame he brings them or is it something else he offers that keeps the connection open? Perhaps we should end this discussion with the line that Gerry revels in,

> *'I wouldn't be me without a camera.' (p.43)*

Roger

Roger Chan is of Malaysian/Filipino descent but he was born in Australia on Australia Day and much is made of this throughout the play. His privileged background and parental expectation are the main focus of his filming. We gradually watch him alter his ambitions to coincide with his lack of success, despite these apparent privileges. Even at the first meeting Cam singles him out for some racist attention and he feels like an outsider throughout the play. He complains about being typecast,

> 'For the last ten years I couldn't go somewhere without somebody staring and pointing. That's him, that's Roger, the Maserati kid. And then on my twenty-first you set me up. And you don't direct my life. I asked you not to show the presents.' (p.42)

Roger is the lost child of the group despite his privilege. He is always searching for something and we see his initial ambition as a child turn into dust as he scrambles to fulfil expectations. His speech at the opening of Scene Twenty-two is revealing in that it shows the pressure he is under, even from Gerry. Later, by the end of Scene Twenty-four, Roger has again changed and talks about a variety of options for his life but concludes by stating,

> 'People tell me I'd be good in the hospitality industry. I play the markets a bit, make money some days. I go clubbing. But the women I like don't go for Asian men, so I end up with...I want to travel, but I wouldn't want to go overseas on my own. What I really like to do is...I get in my car and drive. And I keep driving.' (p.38)

Later Roger's life is spiralling downwards and Gerry sends him away. Roger has lost his money given to him by his father, has been abusing substances and is basically failing at life. He is lonely and Gerry sends him off to 'find himself' and 'grow up'. Roger does go and then seems to haunt Gerry for the rest of the play. We hear of him in Marrakesh then in the newscast when we learn he is being held as a hostage by Karen rebels in Thailand. Roger is murdered but is always alive in a theatrical sense as he is always alive on stage for the audience. In many ways he is Gerry's conscience and he is part of the fitting conclusion to the play as he turns the camera on an unwilling Gerry.

Roger's life changes completely from the little, ambitious seven year old who questions why Gerry would want to make such a documentary to an outcast living in a Buddhist temple in Thailand. His connection with Gerry is certainly strong but not without pain.

Jessie

Jessie is a young girl when we first meet her. Her first words, 'Zoos are bad places' gives us some idea of her thought processes. The significant issue is not her age but her Aboriginality. She moves into being a 'cause junkie' after being motivated by Gerry. Jessie certainly has strong values and we see her at fourteen preparing to go on a march with her parents. Gerry encourages her to speak, to be a leader and she admits if she does it might change her life. Ironically, what Jessie wants at fourteen eventuates as the one thing she can't have,

> 'I want to be all the things that I can be. None of us want that time taken from us. We want our chance at life.' (p.9)

This comment proves to be a foreshadowing. Later in the play Jessie goes to Borneo with Gerry to save the rainforests and later again, continues with her interest in community affairs and causes. She tells Zoe her heart isn't with Gerry earlier yet the others think she is his favourite. In truth the others look to her to lead and often follow her advice, especially when deciding to let Gerry continue. She says she likes her life and is engaged in the world, to the exclusion of any permanent relationship until she meets Theo, the ever tolerant boyfriend, with whom she eventually forms a more permanent relationship, despite Jessie's restless nature.

Jessie's relationship with Gerry is more problematic than any of her other relationships. She likes Gerry and says at one point,

> 'But if Gerry wants to keep going I can't say no. It means too much to him.' (p.34)

In turn, Gerry does seem to favour her, especially with encouragement and then he admits his love for her which seems odd, given he is twenty years her senior. He states,

> *'It's you. I'm interested in the others, I care about them, I like them. But you..I love you. Probably I always have. I mean, since... What does it matter? What matters is I can't get you out of my head. The way you look, the way you think, the fire inside you...'*
> *(p.46)*

Unfortunately or fortunately depending on your perspective Jessie is already pregnant with Theo's baby. Noticeably she doesn't follow Gerry when he leaves. Jessie miscarried but then tells the camera that she doesn't want more children and the energy she might put into children could go to other areas. She and Theo disagree on this and it causes her some conflict but she then heads off to Weipa. Jessie is consistent in her wants and needs throughout the play.

We learn, at the gathering in her and Theo's backyard in 2000, that Jessie has cancer and is to undergo chemotherapy. She allows Gerry to film because she wanted to make Gerry happy but she dies and Theo stops Gerry filming her memorial as he wasn't there for her, just behind the camera. It is over and the unifying force of Jessie is gone. She has had the only real thing she ever wanted taken away from her - 'time'.

Cam

Cameron or Cam as he is known throughout the play is very close to Gerry and is the one who causes Gerry the most angst starting on the first day when he is racist and aggressive. At ten Cam goes to live with his uncle and aunt who have their own kids as his own mother has died. He wants to live with Gerry and this desire reveals a connection has already formed. Cam is obsessed with Australian Rules and doesn't like living with his aunt and uncle. He ends up getting into trouble and Gerry takes him in to help him get his life back together at sixteen. Cam is successful and goes on to have a stellar career, yet his immature streak never leaves him.

We see this immature streak in his behaviour manifest itself in behaviour such as cheating on Annie when she is pregnant, attempting to pick up Zoe and his driving while intoxicated that leads to the accident. He is a lad in the truest sense and Gerry is drawn to this aspect of him. Cam doesn't need the fame that Gerry brings as he is a football hero but he does it for Gerry. He wants his life recorded, even to the point where he is being filmed during the crash. They are in many ways co-conspirators in a boy's life yet Gerry betrays Cam by sleeping with his wife, Annie, after the accident. Gerry tells Roger he helped Cam because,

'he had nobody. Nobody and nothing.' (p.42)

but it is more than this and we learn that Gerry has not released the footage of the night he filmed Cam crash's which destroyed his life. Again, Gerry is manipulating what he wants the public to see and omits himself, despite the high profile of Cam and the value of the footage. We have already read Cam's quote in which he calls Gerry "the devil" but if you haven't read that quote go back now to the section on Gerry and memorise it.

Cam always provides Gerry with great footage and through him Gerry can relive his youth and reject middle age. Cam is forthright and photogenic, creating a great story to follow over the years, yet, as he says, he pays the price and leaves himself with little more than memories and imaginings of what might have been.

Susannah

Susannah is always a little odd and this is reflected in her portrayal. She is precocious as a child and slightly pretentious. She hides a sensitivity and insecurity, despite her academic prowess. Her prediction at the beginning is closest to reality of them all. She wants to be a doctor, singer and a mother with a baby girl and all these eventuate through the play. Susannah gives the impression of always being slightly fragile hidden behind a studied politeness. We see this in her hidden love of poetry. Susannah says at one point she does well at school not because of pleasing her parents but because she has 'standards.' This sums her up well.

Susannah's sensitivity is highlighted in her writing poetry, something she is unsure about,

> *'If I am observant, I think observant is a good thing to be. I try to work out what people are thinking. And feeling. Write? No. I don't write. Yes, I write poetry. No. No, it's too...Can we stop this now?'*
> *(p.13)*

Susannah retains this sense of insecurity and it is repeated in Scene Fourteen when she first reads Gerry some poetry. At this point she is secretly in love with Gerry and this is revealed later when she blatantly breaks her polite manner and states,

*'So now you can fuck me. (Silence) With impunity. Impunity...
I was always the one with the superior vocabulary. I want to fuck
you. Do you want to fuck me?' (p.26)*

Gerry does and then leaves quickly and years later she is still embittered by his seeming rejection. She has an excellent insight into his character when she says,

*'You see what you want to see, when you're shooting. You saw
that silly poem I wrote. You see us all so clearly until you put that
thing down. And then you can't see what you've put on screen for
millions of strangers to see. You can't read your own work.' (p.45)*

Susannah goes overseas to study and work but returns, pregnant and with the aim of working in public health rather than academia. Scene thirty-four is interesting as she talks about her life and happiness. Here Gerry edits her question to him again showing his manipulation and she is very aware of his role in her life. She resents his intrusion into her life at times and this is especially so when he and Zoe want to discuss her daughter Gabrielle's lack of development. She tells him 'I wish I'd never met you.' However, she does continue the filming but doesn't talk as she feels she has 'wrapped it up'.

Susannah seems to have been stifled by her involvement in the project and especially her love for Gerry. She never fulfils her promise in so many ways and the song she repeats in French about the fire going out truly represents her character in so many ways.

Zoe

Zoe is quiet and shy as a child and this is reflected in her stated ambition as a seven year old, "I don't know what I want to be". Zoe is quite lost for much of the shooting until she has her child. Before this she isn't successful academically and leaves school to work in a supermarket because she thinks she is "ordinary". Leaving school opens up life for her in some ways and living with a band makes her think her life has just kicked in "big time". Her life then becomes Alex and the band where she finds some identity. This allows her to escape from the typecast quiet girl from the documentary.

Zoe's pregnancy changes much about her life. She is pregnant to Alex but it is Doug, her lifelong partner, who steps up to fill the paternal or fatherly role and Zoe and Sky become his life. Zoe continues with the filming so Sky can see how they change,

> When I do this now, I'm doing it for my daughter. She'll watch this, even when I'm dead, and she'll know what I was thinking. That's if I know what I'm thinking. 'Not going anywhere'? Is that what I said? I don't remember. I mean, I don't remember her, that girl. I think I'm going somewhere. I don't know where, but somewhere. We'll see. She'll see. My daughter will see. (p.40)

Doug and Zoe form a solid couple and she becomes dependable and secure, even confident. She is strong enough to reject Cam in Melbourne and point out Gerry's deficiencies although there are scars in her life and the secret of Sky's father which is revealed without causing any dislocation to Doug or Sky. It is here that she points out a truth to Gerry that he is the only one who "needs to know the whole story" and that is for the camera, not for any other reason.

Zoe is the one who has the most balanced life by the conclusion of the play. She hasn't done some of the more extraordinary things that the others do but also hasn't suffered as much. Perhaps her typecasting as the quiet one saved her from some of the more extremes of being filmed for her entire life. Zoe finds a purpose in her life, through her child and it expands her in ways that the documentary couldn't.

Doug

Doug is a 'good person' in the truest sense and doesn't want to become involved in the filming as he is aware of Gerry's manipulations. Doug is an intelligent, considerate guy whom Zoe thinks the world of. They have a steady relationship and one that survives the knowledge that he isn't Sky's father. He regrets not continuing law. He states in his first screen appearance,

> *It's the kind of happiness you dream about and suddenly it's yours. No, I didn't finish. That was an independent decision. I wasn't comfortable with the idea of practising law. I'm in the public service. But this is my life. Zoe and Sky. (p.27)*

Doug does admit on camera in Scene Thirty-six that he would go back to law but their financial circumstances wouldn't allow it and Sky comes first. Doug shows his intelligence by being able to reveal Gerry's motives and manipulation as I have touched on earlier. We get conclusive evidence of this in Scene Forty-four when he tells Gerry that he has 'nailed' him as a 'loser' in the footage and the,

> *…perennial job-seeker, the house husband making the casserole, the dad waiting at the school gates, I can wear all that. But to have strangers know that I'm doing it for a child that isn't mine-…That makes me a good story. (p.68)*

Doug doesn't want to participate anymore in Gerry's work and is happy with family snaps. He doesn't want to go on and says clearly "We're no longer a part of this." Doug, as a latecomer to the scene, has a far more objective appraisal and isn't so emotionally attached to Gerry as Zoe. He provides a very different perspective as does our next character, Theo.

Theo

Apollo Theodosopoulos (Theo) is a constant in Jessie's life from 1986 when he follows her after a meeting and offers to feed her. He is patient and persistent and very protective of her despite her reticence in developing the relationship. Eventually they get together as a couple but have a complex relationship because of the miscarriage, her continual need for a cause to follow and then her cancer. He doesn't like Gerry and won't participate in the project despite Gerry trying to convince him. Look carefully at Scene Twenty-five as this explains the divide between Gerry and Theo very clearly. Theo says to him, among other rebuttals,*"Mate. It's not my gig. I'm not in your story"*and he also looks at the camera and says, *"Jess is right. That thing can steal your spirit." (p.39)*

Theo is never happy with Gerry around and cannot see why Jessie continues with the filming, especially the final hospital filming but he acquiesces because he knows Jessie wants to keep Gerry happy. Theo tells Gerry,

> *"She wanted to make you happy. So you took her last moment. You took her death from me, and you took it from yourself. You could have been there." (p.77)*

He refuses to let Gerry film the final scene and walks off with the others leaving Gerry with Roger for the final denouement. Theo is always protective of Jessie. Even when she leaves him to go on another cause, he waits and accepts it despite being unhappy. She cannot see the pain she causes him and he only once expresses it when he calls her a "cause junkie." It is hard not to empathise with Theo who is portrayed positively by Enright. It is interesting that Both Theo and Jessie come from what were seen as marginalised ethnic groups in their community at the time.

Questions for Character

- Is Gerry the protagonist, antagonist or both in the play? Discuss your response with detailed examples from the text. Remember there is no right or wrong answer just supported opinion.

- Discuss how Gerry hides behind the camera and lets the five children/adults live his life for him.

- Do you like Gerry as a character? Give your reasons and in your response include ideas about his editing and inability to stop filming.

- For ONE character discuss how Gerry's filming alters their life.

- Create a character analysis of Roger in one paragraph.

- Discuss the relationship between Roger and Gerry using at least three quotes from the text.

- Why does Roger haunt Gerry? Do you think he is portrayed fairly by Gerry?

- How effective is Roger's return at the conclusion of the play? Think about the final scene of the play and Roger's role in confronting Gerry.

- Create a character analysis of Jessie in one paragraph.

- How does Gerry create adult Jessie in one sense?

- Discuss Jessie's relationship with Theo.

- Why does Jessie play a more dominant role in the play than some of the other children? Discuss Gerry's role in this.

- Do you think Gerry really loves Jessie or is he misinterpreting his emotions and attachment to her?

- Describe Cam as a child. What excuse does Gerry offer for his early behaviour?

- Cam excels at football. How does this success fuel his immature behaviours?

- Why does Annie sleep with Gerry? Analyse Cam's reaction to her infidelity.

- Why does Gerry constantly enable Cam?

- Discuss Cam's relationship with Gerry. Think about issues such as Gerry living through Cam, his inability to tell Cam the truth, his support of Cam in hard times and his behaviour the night of the accident.

- Describe Susannah in one paragraph.

- Analyse the changes in her interactions with Gerry over the course of the play. Try to chart the complexities and the incidents which trigger her different reactions.

- Does her sleeping with Gerry alter their dynamic? Think about how they both respond.

- How do you see Susannah on her return from America?

- Why might she be oblivious to any problems with her child?

- Why might Zoe see herself as 'dumb'?

- Why is her kiss with Jessie so impactful on screen?

- How does Zoe see herself as a teenager?

- Discuss how the birth of Sky changes her life.

- How do you see Zoe at the conclusion of the play? Think about issues such as her new perspective on life, her developing relationship with Doug and her general situation.

- Describe how Doug is perceived through Gerry's filming by the public. Is this a true reflection of him?

- How do you see Doug? Support your ideas with evidence from the text.

- Is Doug correct in wanting to stop Gerry filming and to rely on family snaps to chart their progress? In Doug supplying the shots, how would the issue of control change?

- Discuss Doug's relationship with Zoe. Use at least two quotes from the text to support your ideas.

- Examine Scene Twenty-one where Theo first meets Jessie. What kind of person is Theo portrayed as? Does he change through the play or is his character consistent?

- Discuss Theo's relationship with Jessie. Does it change?

- Analyse the relationship between Theo and Gerry? How do you think they interact with each other?

- Is Theo right to ban Gerry from filming the final goodbye to Jessie on the headland? Support your ideas with evidence form the text.

THEMATIC CONCERNS

Exploring Interactions

Before you read this you should go back and refresh yourself with the rubric and module outline that was included at the beginning of this guide. The questions you will likely be asked will all stem from the rubric and you need to be familiar with this so as you read the text and begin to analyse it, you can jot down ideas, quotes and specific examples to reinforce your ideas. Exploring interactions is basically about the manner in which people live, interact and connect with each other in a variety of situations. The rubric asks for a little more in that it states,

These contexts may include the home, cultural, friendship and sporting groups, the workplace and the digital world. Through exploring their prescribed text and texts of their own choosing, students consider how acts of communication can shape, challenge or transform attitudes and beliefs, identities and behaviours. In their responding and composing, students develop their understanding of how the social context of individuals' interactions can affect perceptions of ourselves and others, relationships and society.

P.14 BOSTES PRESCRIPTIONS DOCUMENT AT

HTTP://WWW.BOARDOFSTUDIES.NSW.EDU.AU/SYLLABUS_HSC/PDF_DOC/ENGLISH-

PRESCRIPTIONS-2015-20.PDF

What this means for our study of Enright's *A Man with Five Children* is that we need to focus on how the characters interact in a variety of contexts and what changes in the way they view the world and others. Obviously, the initial interactions occur when they were children and the initial contacts establish relevance and bonds through shared experiences. This changes over time, not just because each child grows older and has a wider range of life experiences but also because of contextual change. The camera plays a major role in this play of shaping experiences and perceptions, not just in each character's self perception but how they are perceived by others, especially those outside the group. Roger is insistent that this has shaped his life and for a time, Zoe also believes the perception that she is "dumb" is true.

It is impossible to list and explore every individual interaction between characters yet we can establish patterns that may, or may not, vary according to character and circumstance. For example Cam remains consistent in his approach to life and people from the initial impression we have of a loud, rambunctious, opinionated boy who is also bigoted. His interactions change after he is wheelchair bound after the accident and it is with a certain sense of irony that Annie cheats on him as he cheated on her, with Gerry's help.

Susannah remains basically consistent in her interactions. Yet her perspective changes, first after she sleeps with Gerry and then after the birth of her child. When you consider exploring interactions, think about major life events and how they impact characters. This may be a way to link this text to the other related texts that you need to find to enhance your studies.

Another interaction worthy of exploration is the effect of the camera on the perception of the character and how they view the world. Remember that what they say on camera is influenced by how they want to be perceived, although this too, is manipulated by Gerry who films them when they are vulnerable and can't really refuse. For example Cam at the police station, Susannah in the yard with their poetry and Roger at his party with the Maserati in the driveway. Gerry also manipulates perception through how he edits and what he shows. Think about his desire to keep the annual documentary fresh and alive. This brings us to consider Gerry's interactions with the five children and later their partners and children.

We have already examined how Gerry sleeps with one of the three girls and with Annie so those interactions are clear but you can revisit the character section to refresh if you need to. Gerry begins with what seems to be a positive motive,

> *'Five children to speak for young Australia. I hope all five will want to come with me on the journey.' (p.1)*

Here Gerry thinks he is still going to be able to be objective in his approach but, of course, things change as he develops relationships with them and it moves to the subjective and finally the manipulative. He is close, too close, to some of them, indulgent at times and like a father in others. He falls in love, he thinks, with Jessie and eventually he becomes immersed in their lives, entangled to a point where there isn't much else in his.

His interactions lead him to live his life through them, through the lens and he can't give it up. His relationship with the group becomes obsessive and he keeps wanting more, highlighted by his continual need to keep filming precious moments such as Jessie's death rather than interacting on a personal, emotional level. Theo says to him,

> *She wanted to make you happy. So you took her last moment. You took her death from me, and you took it from yourself. You could have been there. (p.77)*

This emotional detachment referred to here is inconsistent with some of his other interactions where he intervenes thus throwing the other characters out emotionally. His interactions with the others leads to his final statement to the camera,

> *Till they turn ... Till they die. One day for the camera to follow them. To a football game, a ballet class, a birthday party, whatever. One day a year for them to speak and be heard. I'd like to be in their lives. Yes, I'd like to be in their lives. No, I'd like them to be in my life. I'd like them to be my life. He is mumbling now. I'd like them to live for me.*

The repetition of the final sentence reverberates through our assessment of Gerry's interactions with the others but is also placed into context by Roger initially asking "But why?" This is also repeated in the final words of the play by the children in unison. Surely there has to be a reason for any interaction, what is Gerry's?

The reason for some interactions in the play is love and these relationships are portrayed carefully and kindly by Enright. We feel for Theo and his kind love for Jessie, despite her inability at times to form a relationship because of the expectations she has grown up with. Doug too is steadfast in his love for his family, despite not being Sky's biological father. Doug is clear in his assessment of Gerry's work and his understanding of family,

> *That makes me a good story. And you'll keep working till you get it. But I won't let you. This story's closed. No more Doug, no more Zoe, no more Sky. See, we're not three separate lives, we're a unit. You mightn't understand that. (p.68)*

This love is portrayed as pure rather than Gerry's type of love which is manipulative, emotionally and personally. When Roger seeks it, Gerry tells him to go because it's not the story he wants. What we can learn here is that when you interact with people even the simplest relationships are complex because of the beliefs and attitudes people bring with them. Communication is complex and there are many variables to consider. Think about the things discussed here and find your own examples that build on them. Examine each of the characters and think about how external factors might reinforce or change them. Cam, for example, immersed in his football culture, would have his behaviour reinforced and supported while a lost Roger has nowhere to turn and has to explore religions overseas to seek peace in himself. Jessie is typecast as a crusader and cannot shake this while Zoe discovers that she can learn and become something more.

It will be your decision about how much the media or the 'digital world' as it is described in the rubric affects these interactions. When you explore interactions in this text there is no shortage of material to examine so use these ideas wisely as a starting point to begin.

Questions on Exploring Interactions

- What, in your opinion, is the most interesting interaction in the play?

- What, in your opinion, is the least interesting interaction in the play?

- Look at the two graphics below. Which do you imagine Gerry to be and why?

- Discuss in detail what the effect of having the children's lives filmed had on their ability to interact. Use ONE character specifically to support your ideas.

- Why might Enright develop specific techniques to show these interactions? In your response show how the playwright's dramatic manipulations allow the audience to interact with the characters in the play.

- How is conflict used to ensure that interactions are interesting? Is this idea of conflict true in real life also?

- Doug states at one point in the play;

  'That makes me a good story. And you'll keep working till you get it. But I won't let you. This story's closed. No more...'

Using this quote as a starting point, discuss how the story needs to be 'good' for Gerry to continue. How much does this drive what he does?

LANGUAGE

Language and Dramatic Techniques

This play should not only been seen as a script but as a performance. We need to examine what and how things are said but also how they are portrayed on stage. The chapter on setting explores how Enright uses the audio-visual element with the large screen dominating the backdrop. It is a reflection of the lives of the children; their realities are portrayed on the screen in edited version. Indeed, they watch their own lives unfold on a yearly basis and millions of people follow and watch them. The show itself must change them as they are celebrities and have to cope with the pressure of that. This screen marries with the ubiquitous camera that Gerry carries around and which he cannot seem to put down.

The camera is a dramatic technique, strongly visual and commented on continuously by the various characters. We need to decide what it represents and I think it conveys Gerry's living his life through the children but also, how subjectively the children are portrayed. One lens, one viewpoint and Enright points out how influential this is in shaping the five lives. Gerry says "It wouldn't be me without the camera" and this is so true. Camera's in our world can be tiny and inconspicuous but this was not so in past decades. We have already noted how it has shaped his life and his relationships and its physical presence on stage is a constant reminder of this. The images the camera shoots are also shown on stage and you need to think of the impact of this backdrop in the theatre.

In regard to this Enright includes many specific stage directions as to what and how things are shown on the screen as well as options. One example is on page 45 when he writes, 'On screen, perhaps an image of Jessie' and, on page 13, THE FIVE CHILDREN 15, watch themselves on screen›. You will find many examples of your own as you read the play. These stagecraft techniques influence an audience's perception of the connections between the characters as they become linked by more than personal contact. The screen and the camera change and manipulate connections and not just between Gerry and the others but between the characters because of how they are perceived.

This perception evolves from what Gerry decides to show and how he manipulates it. I have already commented on the editing process but interactions are shaped by how we perceive people Zoe, for example, comes to see herself not as quiet but as dumb and this influences decisions about her life and who she relates to. Roger is seen as the rich Asian kid whose privileged life gives him every advantage but this is incorrect and he is perceptive enough to see that Gerry has set him up,

> For the last ten years I couldn't go anywhere without somebody staring and pointing. That's him, that's Roger, the Maserati kid. And then on my twenty-first you set me up. And you don't direct my life. I asked you not to show the presents. (p.42)

You will find other examples of this but think about how these manipulations and incorrect perceptions affect how the subjects connect with each other and the world.

The characters have their own method of interacting and their own language style that enables them to connect with the world. We see this early in the play when Enright has to establish separate identities for the characters quickly so the audience can identify with their differences (and similarities). Gerry has the opening monologue which establishes him as the central character aligning all the elements. Roger immediately asks why Gerry is doing this and Cam is outspoken, crude, racist and self-centred; the perfect candidate for television. Susannah's long speech on page 4 establishes her background and intellect while Jessie, who follows her, is more relaxed and engaged with the world. Enright also has Zoe stating

'I don't know what I want to be' (p.5)

This allows for Zoe's life to develop and unfold until she has her own child much later. Once established language remains consistent with some adjustments for age and personal development. We are shocked when Susannah wants to 'fuck' but this wouldn't be inconsistent with Cam and his football slang and colloquialisms such as 'carn'. Susannah maintains her links to the French song while Jessie clearly likes her life as an activist yet this hampers her ability to connect with other people. She finds it hard to have a relationship and we see this in the speech on page 29 and again in her slowly developing relationship with Theo. That language reflects character is seen in the play.

Another factor that connects the subjects is the reunion of the group as they view the screening of the previous show. Here they can explore what each has or has not achieved and follow each other's progress. Despite the passage of time and the movement of characters such as Susannah and Roger overseas we can also follow them due to this staging. Think about how these seemingly disparate people are interacting on stage over time, not an easy task to accomplish in theatrical terms without becoming overly trite, melodramatic or superficial.

It is not just on a language or intellectual level that the connections are formed but on a physical level.

Consider how the sexual connections are formed and how and why Enright allows these to happen in the play. We hear a considerable number of questions being asked throughout the play and these are about life, happiness and the future. One aspect of this is the sexual connections that the characters make. The relationships in the play all seem complex and tainted in some way. We see this in Gerry sleeping with Susannah, Annie and her infidelity, Gerry's 'love' for Jessie, Jessie's relationship traumas with Theo, Doug not being the father of Zoe's daughter, Sky; Roger's penchant for prostitutes and Cam's infidelity. These sexual liaisons seem tawdry at best except for Zoe and Doug. We need to consider why Enright portrays them in this way. The importance of conflict to theatre assumes relevance.

Conflict is central to drama and there must be enough tension and conflict for the audience to be interested. Enright, therefore, needs to develop the connections to keep them intriguing. He must pace events to keep conflict within limits so the narrative doesn't explode or become melodramatic. The sexual tension is emotive and interesting as we do want to know how each of the characters evolve and how they respond to stress. The close proximity of the characters over time adds to these connections and needs. The language in moments is also more emotive as we see the word 'love' bandied about. Another example is Susannah using 'fuck' in an out of character speech and Jessie's use of expletives when she argues with Theo. Also note how the emotive language emerges in times of conflict such as when Theo fights with Jessie in Scene Forty, when Cam argues with Annie and Gerry over her infidelity and when Gerry argues with Roger in Scene Twenty-seven.

As well as identifying the emotive language you should also examine the use of questions and questioning by Enright. Of course Gerry asks questions as a matter of his job description but often the questions, especially those that end scenes, are more focused and raise bigger issues. For example, 'Without a camera?', 'Was she a good kisser? and 'Do you like your life?' It is these little questions that guide us toward the bigger issues in the play and the main focus of our study, exploring interactions which is what we are going to examine in detail in the ideas section of this guide.

Questions on Techniques

- Analyse the use of audio-visual techniques in the play.

- Discuss how the camera becomes a motif in the play but also something more to the audience and the characters in the play.

- Why might Enright use very specific stage directions at times and at other times be more discretionary? In your response use TWO specific examples from the text to support your ideas.

- Describe how, to some extent, character is established through language. In your answer use specific examples from two major characters in the play and one minor character.

- How is one sexual connection made and how does it affect others in the play? How does sexual tension lead to conflict between characters?

- Discuss the use of emotive language in the play. How does it affect the audience's perception of character(s) and why is this kind of language important in the play? Think about stagecraft and the audience in your response.

- Analyse the use of questioning in the play. Why is questioning used as a technique?

- Enright also uses the repetition of ideas and lines to convey his ideas. This technique is common in literature. Why does he use it in the play? Find some examples and analyse two specifically.

ESSAY QUESTION

Read the question below carefully and then examine the essay outline on the following pages. Try to develop your essay along these lines and develop strategies to answer questions that are not essay based.

A list of these alternate response types is given at the end of the sample essay. Look at these. You should be familiar with most of them.

QUESTION

Discuss how A Man with Five Children and one related text explore the interactions between characters within character shaping social frameworks.

THE ESSAY

The essay has been the subject of numerous texts and you should have the basic form well in hand. Ensure you link paragraphs both to each other and back to your argument (which should directly respond to the question). Of course, ensure your argument is logical and sustained.

Make sure you use specific examples and that your quotes are accurate. To ensure that you respond to the question make sure you plan carefully and are sure what relevant point each paragraph is making. It is a solid technique to actually 'tie up' each point by explicitly coming back to the question.

When composing an essay the basic conventions of the form are:

- Introduction - State your argument, outline the points to be addressed and perhaps have a brief definition.

Main Body - A solid structure for each paragraph is:
- Topic sentence (the main idea and its link to the previous paragraph/argument)
- Explanation / discussion of the point including links between texts if applicable.
- Detailed evidence (Close textual reference- quotes, incidents and technique discussion.)
- Tie up by restating the point's relevance to argument / question

- Conclusion - Summary of points
- Final sentence that restates your argument

As well as this basic structure you will need to focus on:

Audience – for the essay the audience must be considered formal unless specifically stated otherwise. Therefore your language must reflect the audience. This gives you the opportunity to use the jargon and vocabulary that you have learnt in English. For the audience ensure your introduction is clear and has impact. Avoid slang or colloquial language including contractions (like doesn't, e.g., etc.).

Purpose – the purpose of the essay is to answer the question given. The examiner evaluates how well you can make an argument and understand the module's issues and its text(s). An essay is solidly structured so its composer can analyse ideas. This is where you earn marks. It does not retell the story or state the obvious.

Communication – Take a few minutes to plan the essay. If you rush into your answer it is almost certain you will not make the most of the brief 40 minutes to show all you know about the question. More likely you will include irrelevant details that do not gain you marks but waste your precious time. Remember an essay is formal so do not do the following: story-tell, list and number points, misquote, use slang or colloquial language, be vague, use non sentences or fail to address the question.

ESSAY OUTLINE – *A MAN WITH FIVE CHILDREN*

Discuss how A Man with Five Children and one related text explore the interactions between characters within character shaping social frameworks.

A few notes about the question:

- Remember the question is asking you what you have learned about the formation of interactions in the play, within the framework of the longitudinal study and documentary. Then explore how the relationships are portrayed using appropriate documentary and dramatic techniques.

- It is important you take note of the ideas the statement raises and check your response addresses them.

- Take care you use the number of texts the examiner asks for. There is no value in writing on more than one related text and you will definitely be penalised for writing on less.

- You MUST have quotations and textual references that show you have a good knowledge and understanding of your prescribed AND one other text.

- Your response must look at BOTH WHAT the texts have taught you about the importance of exploring interactions AND HOW the composer represented those ideas.

PLAN: Don't even think about starting without one!

Introduce...

The texts you are using in the response

Definition:

Explanation of exploring interactions, the social context and its impact in the texts

- Argument: *A Man with Five Children* and one ORT is able to communicate these interactions:
- Between people
- They are changed by context etc.

You need to let the marker know what texts you are discussing. You can start with a definition but it could come in the first paragraph of the body. You MUST state your argument in response to the question and the points you will cover as part of it. Don't wait until the end of the response to give it!

Idea 1- People interact and change how they see others and the world

- explain the idea
- where and how shown in *A Man with Five Children* and one Related text
- relevance to modern audiences

Idea 2- People interact in different ways depending on context etc.

- explain the idea
- where and how shown in *A Man with Five Children* and one Related text
- Explain techniques i.e. how.
- relevance to modern audience

You can use the things you have learned to organise the essay. For each one you say where you saw this in your prescribed text and where in the other text.

Two ideas are usually enough as you can explore them in detail.

- Summary of two key ideas
- Final sentence that restates your argument

Make sure your conclusion restates your argument. It does not have to be too long.

EXPLORING INTERACTIONS: OTHER RELATED TEXTS

PROSE FICTION

Town by James Roy (2007)

Thirteen interwoven short stories from thirteen different adolescents set over thirteen months in an unnamed Australian country town. This text explores the interactions of these young adults in a school and a wider community setting. Dealing with contemporary hard hitting issues such as disability, family, death and grief, racism and sexuality. We slowly begin to see how these characters' own world is shaped by their peers around them through interactions both great and small.

A Long Way Down by Nick Hornby (2005)

Four strangers meet on New Year's Eve on top of a London building where they plan to jump and end their lives. However, the four instead form a sort of surrogate family that helps them stay alive and work through their issues. This text uses multiple viewpoints to delve deeper into each character's psyche and propel the plot forward. It is through the interactions of four very different people we begin to explore how these people transform their view on the world and set themselves free from dark places.

Deadly, Unna? by Phillip Gwynne (1998)

This novel explores cross cultural interactions and uses the game of Australian Rules Football to explore racism in a small South Australian coastal town. The novel also explores the interaction between sporting life and community life and how they play into one another. As the novel progresses we see understanding of the other raise in our protagonist, while racial tensions come to a head with other characters. The novel manages to blend sport with a relevant social message that stresses the importance of communication in order for positive change to happen.

Gone Girl by Gillian Flynn (2012)

A compelling crime thriller that moves its plot along through the viewpoint of two main characters. As we watch the two interact through a series of first-hand experiences and diary entries we begin to unravel this complicated mystery. Character interactions are multi-faceted and we start to realise everyone is not who they seem. This is a text that explores the complicated relationships between human beings and how different forms of communication can be used to manipulate one another.

The Slap by Christos Tsiolkas (2008)

At a family BBQ a man slaps a child who is not his own, what follows is eight viewpoints that show the effects of that one incident and how it has changed lives/interactions/relationships forever. This text explores the new multi-cultural Australia and how one incident can shape us and the way we see the world. The author is interested in how a very different group of people from different cultures, religions, sexualities and belief systems learn to live and interact with one another when they all have a different opinion on what is right and what is wrong.

FILM

Crash *directed by Paul Haggis (2004)*

A film about social and racial tensions that takes course over two days in Los Angeles, as we see several character's stories interweave and interact with one another. The interactions between these characters force the audience to question racial stereotypes while at the same type acknowledge the truth that some of these stereotypes contain.

As the title suggests, the film shows its characters colliding and crashing, sometimes metaphorically and sometimes literally and it is through these interactions a bleak, yet realistic portrait of humanity is painted.

American Beauty *directed by Sam Mendes (1999)*

An American drama that looks deeper into the seemingly normal suburban life of several characters. Marital and generational conflict is explored as we look closer at the lives of these people and their interactions with one another.

The film exposes the flaws of the 'American Dream' and how the lack of meaningful interaction and connection can lead to isolation. The film also fantastically juxtaposes a variety of both positive and negative connections between characters and explores their impacts on these people.

Lars and the Real Girl *directed by Craig Gillespie (2007)*

A delusional young man, Lars, strikes up a romantic relationship with a doll he finds on the internet. Lars struggles to interact and relate to the community around him but manages to find a meaningful existence with this plastic doll. Through the interaction between Lars and the doll and the way the community interact with Lars and accepts this strange situation, the importance of community, compassion and the importance of understanding one another is revealed.

Her *directed by Spike Jonze (2013)*

Set in the not so distant future, an introverted man, Theodore, sparks up a relationship with an advanced artificially intelligent operating system. What starts as a friendship soon turns to love. While many texts explore how technology is making it harder for us to interact with one another, this film shows how technology can connect us on a level deeper than ever before. Through the interaction between Theodore and the operating system "Samantha" we learn that technological interactions can not only strengthen relationships but fulfil emotional needs.

PICTURE BOOK

John Brown Rose and the Midnight Cat- *Jenny Wagner, Ron Brooks*

The following site may be useful in considering the interactions within this beautiful book. *http://annabranford.com/uncategorized/john-brown-rose-and-the-midnight-cat*

The Lost Thing - Shaun Tan

This is about interactions and lack of interactions. If you do not know the work of Shaun Tan, it is worth exploring. Also consider The Rabbits.

SONGS

When selecting songs for a related texts. Students are reminded to analyse lyrics and musical style and features.

Father and Son *written and performed by Cat Stevens (1970)*

A song that explores generational difference and conflict through interaction in form of a conversation between a father and son who hold very different views about life and what can be gained from life. The listener is presented with two distinct voices and listen to both men express their indifference towards one another. Stevens uses tone of voice perfectly to paint two different characters and showcase the generational differences that occur and how we can challenge what others believe.

URL Badman *written and performed by Lily Allen (2014)*

A contemporary pop song that explores interactions between young people, specifically young men who sit at home on the internet attacking others. Allen uses satire, sarcasm, wit and contemporary references to poke fun at the cyber culture that belittles others safely behind a computer screen and keyboard.

She exposes the meaningless interactions that occur online and hits back at cyber bullying.

SHORT FILM

***Look Up** by Gary Turk (2014) – YouTube*
A short film that utilises spoken word and visual techniques to warn us of the dangers of the digital culture. The narrator stresses that we no longer interact with one another in reality but more with our digital devices, and by doing this we are missing out on the world around us and an abundance of experiences.

Using irony, Turk expresses how inventions that were designed to connect us, have actually isolated us more and he believes we need to get back to more meaningful interactions that are based in reality.

***Just A Friend** by Sophia Thakur and Chozen (2013)*
A short film that uses poetry and spoken word to explore the interaction between a young couple that are experiencing an issue that affects many couples, trust. Using poetic language the couple express their feelings toward each other and if they can trust each other. We watch them interact and follow their body language, facial expressions and other visual techniques, using these as further clues to piece their interaction together and whether or not they can get through their problems.

With thanks to Michael Ursino